SCAPE

The Poiema Poetry Series

Poems are windows into worlds; windows into beauty, goodness, and truth; windows into understandings that won't twist themselves into tidy dogmatic statements; windows into experiences. We can do more than merely peer into such windows; with a little effort we can fling open the casements, and leap over the sills into the heart of these worlds. We are also led into familiar places of hurt, confusion, and disappointment, but we arrive in the poet's company. Poetry is a partnership between poet and reader, seeking together to gain something of value—to get at something important.

Ephesians 2:10 says, "We are God's workmanship . . ." *poiema* in Greek—the thing that has been made, the masterpiece, the poem. The Poiema Poetry Series presents the work of gifted poets who take Christian faith seriously, and demonstrate in whose image we have been made through their creativity and craftsmanship.

These poets are recent participants in the ancient tradition of David, Asaph, Isaiah, and John the Revelator. The thread can be followed through the centuries—through the diverse poetic visions of Dante, Bernard of Clairvaux, Donne, Herbert, Milton, Hopkins, Eliot, R. S. Thomas, and Denise Levertov—down to the poet whose work is in your hand. With the selection of this volume you are entering this enduring tradition, and as a reader contributing to it.

—D. S. Martin
Series Editor

COLLECTIONS IN THIS SERIES INCLUDE:

Six Sundays toward a Seventh by Sydney Lea
Epitaphs for the Journey by Paul Mariani
Within This Tree of Bones by Robert Siegel
Particular Scandals by Julie L. Moore
Gold by Barbara Crooker
A Word In My Mouth by Robert Cording

Scape

poems

LUCI SHAW

CASCADE *Books* • Eugene, Oregon

SCAPE
Poems

The Poiema Poetry Series

Cascade Books
An Imprint of Wipf and Stock Publishers
199 W. 8th Ave., Suite 3
Eugene, OR 97401

www.wipfandstock.com

ISBN 13: 978-1-62564-179-3

Cataloging-in-Publication data:

Shaw, Luci.

Scape : poems / Luci Shaw ; with a Foreword by Eugene H. Peterson.

xiv + 78 p.; 23 cm.

The Poiema Poetry Series

ISBN 13: 978-1-62564-179-3

1. Poetry. 2. Christian poetry, American. I. Peterson, Eugene H., 1932–. II. Title. III. Series.

PS3569 H384 S15 2013

Manufactured in the USA

"Feather" engraving used with permission by Barry Moser.

Scape

BOTANY: a plant stem growing directly from the ground
BIOLOGY: a stalk-like part such as the shaft of a feather
ARCHITECTURE: a stake, column or support

Also by Luci Shaw:

Poetry
Listen to the Green
The Secret Trees
Postcard from the Shore
Polishing the Petoskey Stone
Writing the River
The Angles of Light
The Green Earth
Waterlines
What the Light Was Like
Harvesting Fog

For children
The Genesis of It All

Anthologies edited
Sightseers into Pilgrims
A Widening Light
Accompanied by Angels

With Madeleine L'Engle
Wintersong
A Prayer Book for Spiritual Friends
Friends for the Journey

Festschrift
The Swiftly Tilting Worlds of
*   Madeleine L'Engle*

Non-fiction prose
God in the Dark
Water My Soul
The Crime of Living Cautiously
Breath for the Bones
Adventure of Ascent (forthcoming)

Musical settings by
Alice Parker
Alan Cline
Frederick Frahm
Roland Fudge
Knut Nystedt
Ed Henderson

Contents

Acknowledgments | x
Foreword by Eugene H. Peterson | xi

Botanicals | 1

So It Is With the Spirit | 3
Signals | 4
The Slow Pleasures | 5
The Birthday Flowers | 6
Old Hand | 7
At the Clinic | 8
The Promise | 9
The Green Shiver | 10
Flowerhead | 11
Still Life | 12
Reading Lesson | 13
Deconstruction | 14
Thunder and Then | 15
The God Fruit | 16
Announcements | 17

Biologicals | 19

Catch of the Day | 21
Chiang Mai | 22
Mailbox | 23
Novel | 24

Contents

A Robin in the Late Afternoon | 25

Sparrow | 26

Meeting Your Match | 27

Incarnate | 28

Engine | 29

Under the Skin | 30

Open End | 31

Sonnet for My Left Hip | 32

What in the Wind? | 33

The Window | 34

Knitting in the Wild | 35

Good Friday | 36

Collection, Recollection | 38

The Golden Carp | 39

Invasion | 40

Credo | 41

The Possibilities of Clay | 42

To Be a Bird | 43

Architectures | 45

Scaling the Rocks | 47

Three Dimensions | 48

Cave Art | 49

Unseen | 50

Ec-stasis | 51

The Moon in Advent | 52

Singing About God in Church | 53

What the Morning Says to Her | 54

What to Do with Bits of String | 55

Soft Rock | 56

Trend | 57

Destination | 58

Lakeway Drive | 59

What I Needed to Do | 60

Verb | 61

Under Cover | 62

States of Being | 63

Contents

Singularities | 64

Compline at the Cathedral | 66

Spire | 67

Dancing in the Cathedral | 68

Epiphany | 69

Mary Considers Her Situation | 71

Getting It Right | 73

Iron | 74

Emmaus Road Remembered | 75

Secure | 76

Translation | 77

Acknowledgments

The Anglican Theological Review: "The Moon in Advent"

Art House America (blog): "What the Morning Says to Her"

Books & Culture: "The Golden Carp," "At the Clinic," "To Be a Bird," "Compline," "Incarnate"

The Christian Century: "Soft Rock," "Knitting in the Wild," "Dancing in the Cathedral," "Catch of the Day"

Conversations: "What to Do with Bits of String," "The God Fruit"

Crux: "The trend" "Emmaus Road Remembered"

Laity Connection: "Frio River"

The Other Journal: "Translation," "Invasion"

The Pinyon Review: "Chiang Mai," "Under the Skin"

Ruminate: "So It Is with the Spirit"

Vineyards: "Flowerhead," "Mailbox"

Weavings: "Safe," "What God Says to a Street Person in Our Town"

Foreword

I first met Luci Shaw in Chicago something like forty years ago at a gathering in which she read some of her poems. I've been listening to and reading her poems ever since. The first poem I memorized after meeting her was *Royalty,* a Luci Shaw poem that uses words of utter simplicity to etch the profundities of incarnation unforgettably.

> He was a plain man
> and learned no Latin
>
> Having left all gold behind
> he dealt out peace
> to all us wild men
> and the weather
>
> He ate fish, bread,
> country wine and God's will
>
> Dust sandaled his feet
>
> He wore purple only once
> and that was an irony.

(*Listen to the Green,* 1971 Wheaton Il: Harold Shaw Publishers)

Now, after a lifetime of writing poetry she is still at the top of her game in this new gathering of poems, well described by the poet laureate of the Bible as "still bringing forth fruit in old age, / ever full of sap and green" (Ps. 92.14).

Poets, the gifted ones at least, are conspicuously gifted and imaginative in their use of metaphor. My own vocation as pastor has been largely spent in encouraging and training men and women under my care in the reading of the Holy Scriptures and taking these Scriptures seriously as the living truth of God and his ways. But "seriously" in our present-day reading culture very often means literally. Science provides the standard by which we judge truth. Truth is what can be verified under laboratory conditions. Truth is what is empirically true—with things it is what we can test and probe, measure and weigh—with language it is what can survive strenuous logical analysis. It is what we often refer to as "literal."

But metaphor is a form of language that cannot pass such logical scrutiny, cannot make it through the laboratory tests. Unfortunately for the literalists (and fortunately for the rest of us) the Bible is chock full of metaphor, which means that if we assume that "literal" is the only means to be "serious" we are going to be in trouble much of the time. For a metaphor is literally a lie.

A metaphor states as true something that is literally not true. For instance, "God is a rock," a frequent Hebrew assertion about God ("The Lord is my rock . . . Who is a rock, except our Lord?" Ps. 18:2, 31). If we take the sentence literally, instead of going to church on Sunday mornings to worship, we will visit the local stone quarry and shop for a god rock that we can erect in our backyard. The alternative is to dismiss the sentence as meaningless, which would leave us with a Bible with every other sentence or so deleted.

The metaphor treated literally is simply absurd. But if we let it have its way with us, it pushes us to clarity at a different level. So why not say it plainly? Tell it to us straight? Denise Levertov in her poem "Poetics of faith" tells us why:

"Straight to the point"
      can ricochet,
            unconvincing.

Circumlocution, analogy,
      parables, ambiguities, provide
            context, stepping-stones.

(*The Stream and the Sapphire*, NY: New Directions. 1997, 31)

For one thing, God's action and presence among us is so beyond our comprehension that sober description and accurate definition are no longer functional. The levels of reality here are so beyond us that they require metaphor that calls on the imagination to participate in the extensive reality that we all inhabit but cannot weigh or explain or measure, which includes most of what deals with the soul and God. Without metaphor we are ill-equipped to respond or enter into what we cannot see, cannot hear, cannot feel.

That is why poets are so essential for all of us who are dealing with God and the Scriptures—to provide us with imagination that can enter into what cannot be seen or even entered into our hearts. And that is why Luci Shaw serves the Kingdom of God so well at this time in our history. As in this poem, *Reading Lesson* from this volume.

> The forest is a library of trees
> whose books, in autumn, open
> for our education to its pages,
> leaves that turn and turn, under
> the air's inquiring fingers.
>
> On the ground, light and shadow.
> The maples drop their syllables until
> the grass burns with words.
> I pick up one, two, to take home.
> Together they spell "Glory."

But preference for the literal among many has a stubbornly long life. I have come to believe that it is an unthinking preference. My experience as parent supplemented by my experience as a pastor cautions me that the peril of the literal is that it ignores the inherent ambiguities in all language, takes the source language prisoner and force-marches it, shackled and chained into an English that nobody living speaks. The language is lobotomized—the very quality that gives language its genius, its capacity to reveal what we otherwise would not know, is excised, extreme literalism insists on forcing each word into a fixed immovable position, all the sentences strapped into a straitjacket. I now see why Luther, the grandfather of Reformation translators, did not take kindly to the critics who bashed his vernacular translation. He called them "those lemmings the literalists."

That accounts for my own practice of over fifty years now of assigning poets for remedial reading among those whom I encourage in a receptive, imaginative, and participatory reading of Holy Scripture and practice of prayer. And it is why I am particularly pleased to have in my hands yet another gathering of Luci Shaw's poems to stimulate this kind of reading and praying, thoughtfully metaphorical, that weds the invisible and visible—all the operations of the Trinity—in a comprehensive embrace.

Eugene H. Peterson
Professor Emeritus of Spiritual Theology
Regent College, Vancouver, B.C.

Botanicals

So It Is With the Spirit

How secretly the bones move
        under the skin
and the veins thread their way
        through their forests, the trees
of bones, the mosses of cells,
        the muscle vines.
How privately the ears
        tune themselves to music heard
only in the echoing cave of the head.
        And the tongue in its grotto tests
the bitterness of unripe fruit, and wine,
        the mouth feel of honey in the comb.
How cunningly our shadows
        follow us as we walk.
And our breath, how it moves in
        and out without great thought.
Even rain, which needs no summons from us
        but flows, a gift from heaven,
as the grasses rise greenly, shivering.
        Just so, beauty besieges us
unannounced, invading us, saving our souls.
        So it is with the Spirit.

Signals

Like my own
effortless breathing,

my neighbor's faded
prayer flags twitch.

Roadside grasses
flurried by a speeding truck

send their
negligible signals

day and night
obedient to their universe—

its nudge of air. No response
expected.

With a flick of the heart I send
my own messages up,

and wait for answers.

The Slow Pleasures

So, the words come slowly, like
the minutes in an hour, or even
the hours in a day—one by one.

In the cave of your mouth they taste
like oranges, green melons. Each offers its own
tang, its own unhurried flush that glazes

your tongue. A delicious vowel flourishes
there, rounding, a flame struck by the match of
a fricative, a plosive, a sibilant—C, V, P, S, T, Z.

Each mouth sound knows this is not its end;
that even after being swallowed,
mated, subsumed, essences persist.

For now, let them re-echo in porcelain,
crimson, onion, ivory, ovary, zither.
Allow each the slow pleasure of being.

The Birthday Flowers

You hope that moisture
will surge again up the green
stalks and flesh out
the lily petals' crumpled,
browning skin.

So, you change the water,
cut the stems at a clean angle,
add a bit of sugar, as if
mixing a drink for yourself
as well as the flowers.

Mums always last the longest.
Before that, you pluck
out the rosebuds, their pink
heads hanging, shamed for
their failure to revive.

The ferns' fronds are
resilient, but eventually
they shrivel. And you are left with
the container, Made In England
stamped on its ivory base.

Old Hand

The plum blue veins embroider their way
through a shrinkage of tissue, a lacing
of vines sucking at an unseen reservoir.
I touch my parchment skin, pushing it sideways
with the gentle forefinger of the other hand,
and the pale tendons gleam like ivory
over the backdrop of murky muscle.

Across a keyboard the fingers flicker,
dedicated, busy with words that are concentrating
on imaginings larger than hinged metacarpals
or a minor mountain range of knuckles.
Made for work, curving to the keys, necessary adjuncts
to language, bridges from the brain.

At the Clinic

On a scale of one to ten. . . .
The doctor leans towards me
with his pad of paper, needing to
record a number for my pain.

I tell him, four for my shoulder;
my hip joint, eight; my knee—
not sure, changes with
the weather. . . .

It's the old conundrum—
how to add up my complaints
for his chart? Say—seventeen?

His difficulty's ancient—
how to feel another's hurt
and classify it, while my prayers
for relief rise like thorns.

The Promise

Follow the path that the Lord your God has
commanded you, that you may live long in
the land you possess. —DEUT. 5:33

In Mendocino County we stopped for
a wine-tasting. The hills were radiant with
light and fruit. After lunch at the vineyard cafe
we bought a dry white and walked
the rows of grapevines held up on
their supports, old men on crutches.

Business was sparse that day. *Want to see*
something weird? the owner asked. We clambered
down to a cave a hundred feet under the slope,
and felt in the earthy dark a tangle of root fibers.
A flashlight gleamed, and the beards
of the ancients lit up like live wires.

The Green Shiver

The forest floor bleak, choked
with a winter's leaves, and winter wet.
Against the evidence, buds on the wild dogwoods
glisten, listen for a signal, lining up
for bloom-time—when to burst and who'll
be first? Every year, it's according
to weather, the wait for the heat-throb,
wind fresh through the naked
birch trunks longing to get green.
The pressure's on, like listening for a
starter pistol, finger on the trigger.

Spring is wound tight enough to let go
any minute. Overarching the ravine,
the cedars start their annual scatter of yellow
sexual dust for the next generation.
The clematis resists her tedium of withered brown,
cancels her winter sleep with a vertical thrust
up the trellis, like a slow shooting star.

How can we help but hope, sprouts
urged to fulfill a kind of promise—
a covenant with the world, that in unfolding,
leaf tips flaring up and out, woody hearts pregnant
with bloom and blessing, we will drink rain, light,
heat for our emerald living. We face the sun
full on—its lavish encouragement for cold to lift,
shift, and move away. Holding on, ready for
that shiver, a sliver of thrill like a jade thread
through a labyrinth, when within us
something fresh and green explodes.

Flowerhead

When she wasn't embroidering tablecloths
our grandmama crocheted doilies
for breakfast trays, tatted antimacassars
for the back of his upholstered chair
to protect the fabric from
my grand-dad's ancient, oily head.

His vision of heaven dimmed, he missed
the midnight stars and fireworks on
the Fourth. In July, at ninety-two,
even broad daylight showed him
only the misty coverlet of Queen Anne's lace
on the meadow.

No matter how lovely, age happens.
Come fall, this flowered field
will bend its thin bones from stars
to wired cages for small insects,
the browned flowerets bowing to the center
venerating each other's spent life.

Still Life

Occasionally
I'd like to arrange
a still life
and then
go live in it—
an artful pot,
dried flowers,
a stone frog
whose eyes
never blink,
and perfect calm.

Reading Lesson

The forest is a library of trees
whose books, in autumn, open
for our education to its pages,
leaves that turn and turn, under
the air's inquiring fingers.

On the ground, light and shadow.
The maples drop their syllables until
the grass burns with words.
I pick up one, two, to take home.
Together they spell "Glory."

Deconstruction

When I try to carve in air
an outline of what was there,
a memory of presence, I can only
think about absence.

When we built our new
house on the hillside next to
the giant Douglas fir,
the machines dug deep for
a foundation so that the naked roots
stuck out like live wires, knowing
air and sky for the first time.

Tall enough to be
unsafe in a high wind, they said,
like a green sail on the Bay,
heeling over at the will of any gust.

We knew then, we and our neighbors,
what had to be done. It was murder.
The saws took only an hour to erase
the splendid sound of wind through needles,
the landmark muscle of trunk.

In the hollow at the base,
as was their custom, the deer
would have given birth.

Thunder and Then

Thunder and then the rain comes and the
prairie that has been baked dry and the
shriveled grass and the ground that has
thirsted all summer open like mouths as
the wet arrives at first in whispers and
then in sheets of silver arrows that tear the
air and join like the clapping of hands to
a downfall that makes splashes in the dirt
and grows to pools that shine in the silver light
and the dry creeks with their stones begin to
thank God for sending water for their need
so that there is praise in the rushing streams
and the trees also raise praise with their leaves
flashing and now wind like a fist takes hold of the
house and shakes it and us and it seems that
all the world is drowning in the delight of deluge.

The God Fruit

And lo, it came upon me that
though my thoughts of my Beloved
rose no higher than the flight
of a sparrow, and that I felt
deprived of the holy union
that I sought therein, of a sudden
a gleam arrived and I saw it
as through a morning mist, and it was
borne in upon me that the loving
thoughts of the Mighty One
were falling upon me like ripe fruit,
golden apples dropping into
the glass bowl that was my soul, and I
was enlightened and filled with joy.

Announcements

I watch them arrive singly. It's like
hearing the brief, high yelp of a kid

just let out of school, bounding across
the sunlit playground.

Today this gray world's drop of color settles
on a bird with a pomegranate breast.

In the supermarket parking lot
a lady bug stationed on someone's windshield.

The first bee on the heather that will soon
be ripe with purple and hum.

My clematis sending its green shooting star
up the trellis like a nerve touched by fire.

Biologicals

Catch of the Day

It leaps, breaking the skin of the lake
of possibility, this thing that flashes steel—
this trout of a poem, wild with life, rainbow scales
and spiny fins. Now, for patience, the pull of the catch:

I cast, wait for the tug—the jerk of hook in bony jaw—
feel the line go taut. The ballet begins, a wrestle
to land this flailing, feral thing—all thrash and edge—
and tame it into telling its own muscular story.

I heave it over the rim of its arrival, glorious,
fighting the whole way, slippery as language.
Its beauty twitches on the floor boards, its glisten
spilling over the lip of my notebook page.

Chiang Mai

In his time off, my doctor son
        forgets bodies,
carves spoons. With surgical precision
        he uses his little curved scalpel,
and though the wood is raw
        and the shavings fall like leaves
on the floor around him,
        no blood is shed.

I'm watching the slow reveal:
        sculpting, he uncovers
the spoon-shape within
        the blunt stick that he
used to defend himself today,
        chasing away the wild dogs
on his morning run. Now he is renewed
        for tomorrow's long hours
at the clinic, treating the bleeding bodies
        and their resident souls.

Mailbox

Yesterday—half a block down our street
the mail arrived. And today, here I am again,
hopeful as ever for possibility—a postcard
from Fez? A flat box with a book in it? A small check?
But this morning, disgust: just five catalogs—
flaunting red bikinis, coffee grinders, hiking boots—
that have cost some trees their green lives.

How cries and answers are strung together
with expectation resilient as wires, reinforced
by delay—the spider, alert at the heart of her silk circles;
the nest and her bird; a summer cottage waiting vainly
all summer to be cluttered with damp swim suits and sand;
this yawning mailbox with our street number on it;
this mailbox with nothing in it, calling out its need.

Novel

I'm utterly engrossed in the turn of
plot when a tiny visitor shows up, strolling
down the page, halting briefly at an
interesting word ("limbo"). She is, quite literally,
small as a pin head with eight feathery legs
like bits of dust. And dust is her color;
I'm guessing she's too young to be fashionable.

When she clambers over the page edge
I turn the book over and there she is, silhouetted
against a patch of red on the cover. Evidently
finding celebrity endorsements uninspiring,
she rejoins me on the printed page, smaller
than the letter "o" in *on,* on which she sits and
considers the impregnability of a preposition.

We read together for a while, stunned
by the power of fiction. I need to turn
the page, but I can't. She's still barricaded
in her "o", and it's against my principles
to squash a friend. I lay the book down, open.
Hours later I check back but she's gone, off
to think up her own plot, or plan her first web.

A Robin in the Late Afternoon

The window's open, so I hear
each crystal note. Even with eyes closed,
I know a robin when I hear one,
telling the air between us how happy he is
about the soft rain and its summons
to the worms in the dark underground.

A pause. And then he sings again
from a more distant branch, but just as clear.
Or is it his mate? No matter, it's a robin song,
a shower for the heart. I am no worm.
I do not tunnel under sod. But I am called,
beckoned into fresh hopefulness.
Bless God for birds, their vowels
pure and persuasive as spring rain.

Sparrow

This undistinguished, indistinguishable bird—
this prototype of insignificance—
this very moment's sparrow at
our porch feeder—makes of her compactness
a virtue. From between the wires
she pecks the black sunflower seeds, neat head bobbing,
purposeful, economical, precise.
Watchful—peck and peek, peck and check.

I have seen scarlet tanagers, purple finches,
grosbeaks, red-footed gulls, even the arrogant
displays of peacocks. In her anonymity,
this diminutive bird is who she is, her suit
brown-grey as damp dust, eyes bright as beads.
This simple-ness, this pure unselfconsciousness,
this understated . . . this. . . . Oh, the adjectives multiply,
but they are too large for this small one,
who humbles my own mud-brown heart.

She poises her nimble self to flick away, quick
as scissors—at a cat, a squirrel,
my movement at the glass door.

I tilt my head for a better angle, and she's gone,
to the safety of the cedars.

Sometimes in my timidity I overcompensate
and try to sound large until I know
such falsehood betrays him who humbled himself,
who values a sparrow.

Meeting Your Match

The morning river so still, just listening
for any twitch of sight or sound, so that when
the early fisherman casts his line, its tautness
is answered at the surface by a partner,
a clean angle, meeting in a flawless mirror kiss.

And we, in some odd, unlikely time
tug on that line that plunges deep and finds
its companion mind lurking among
the lily stems.

Incarnate

Now crowding down
time's alleys, he's immense,
a thunderhead—
then, on the sly,
bright as a blood petal,
slight as a wheat seed,
insinuating into our living,
so that unexpectedly
our dumb mouths
speak him. Our fingers
acknowledge a dexterity
beyond our own.
Even as we stagger
our limbs turn fleet
as goats. Our myopia
suddenly clears
as he begins to open us
to what we're meant to see—
his tenderness as he
judges the brownness
of the egg before it is laid,
tells a candle how long
to burn, designs the coil
of the snail in his small
house, and the trail
of glisten that shows
where God led him.

Engine

For so long it has done its secret work,
my faithful heart—a fist-sized knot
closing and opening, clenching and pulsing.
Its names are *Patience* and *Perseverance*.
Its other name is *Mortality*.

What can a heart do but keep pumping?
Sometimes it jumps, misses a beat, races,
feels uncertain of itself for a few seconds
then sends the blood to throb in my throat.
The doctor gave me a pill for that,
but I don't ever hope to have a heart
that doesn't leap with astonishments too big
to contain, bigger than fireworks on the Fourth.

Under the Skin

I look along my arm, lean,
brown from summer, the pale hairs lit
by late afternoon. Inside
are bones that I have never met,
and blood vessels teeming in the hidden meat—
the rivers in my map.

Consider bark, and the veiled life
of trees. At night, while we sleep,
the arterial hum of xylem and phloem
fills the forest like an anthem—
sap rising and falling, thick
with life, feeding leaves the way
the surprises of being drench the heart.

But down in our ravine, under the membrane
of the running stream, who knows
what ignites the golden pebbles,
stirring them to dance among
the splinters of light?

Open End

Wound, tight as wire in our
mortality, we watch, bemused,
as the spring uncoils. Everything
morphs to a dream of history,

the memory of a memory,
the way music fades as we
turn a corner, dims
with every mounting step.

Reading our lives is like
reading beach sand, or an hourglass—
an open-ended novel before
the final draft, the manuscript

half-typed, not yet submitted—
the character not fully realized,
the loose ends adrift, the conflicts
never quite resolved.

Sonnet for my Left Hip

I felt an ache that sleeping could not drown.
It ran from my left hip joint to my mind—
nagged at my thinking as I drove in town.

All night I'd shifted in my thin nightgown
to find a pose to rest in. Now I find
pain stabs me climbing up or reaching down.

Why does this symptom, heavy as a stone,
quicken to a darkness for my mind
to niggle at? It's likely just a bone

That calcified and brought my mind around
to fears of diminution. We're all destined
for aching as the world is round,

Though I can't find the words to tell you how
it hurts, or why it came, or what it feels like now.

What in the Wind?

This was a gale that formed like a fist,
a punch turning into a full kick that almost
sent me flying down the hill. The Greek word
translates as *a movement of air*, but this
was karate. I loved the force of it, its full
release and enthusiasm.

In my tedium, I wish I might
keel over when that other spirit blows, or that
that fierce, holy breath would fill me to
almost bursting, a red balloon
buoyant with air, pressure inside and out,
and no strings attached.

The window

looked so fine,
washed to a shine
but today this
small bird killed
herself against it.

She fell, feathers
awry
all frilled.
I thought, maybe
just stunned,
unfit to fly,

until, stilled,
a warmth soft
in my hand,
I knew she was
undone.

Her eye, a bead
unblinking.
She was so small,
brown
and mid-gray.
She went down,
victim of our need
for clarity
and a view
of the bay.

Knitting in the Wild

Douglas Fir campground, Oct. 2012

The pale bits—twigs, fibers,
pine needles—sun-struck,
fall through the lazy air
as if yearning to be embodied in
my knitting, like gold flecks woven into
a ceremonial robe.

Then surprise—a new marvel!
Like a parachutist, a very small beetle
lands on the greeny stitch I have just
passed from left needle to right;
the creature's burnished carapace
mirrors precisely the loop of glowing,
silky yarn he has chosen.

When this shawl ends up
warming someone's shoulders,
will she sense the unexpected—
this glance, this gleam,
this life spark?

Good Friday

for Joyce Peasgood,
who taught us how to decorate Ukrainian Easter eggs

By invitation, on Good Friday
we find our places at her dining table
for a feast of small miracles. The dye baths
readied—scarlet, saffron, aquamarine,
mustard yellow and a green deep as
a Ukrainian forest. A legacy of patterning
becomes the sign of reversal as three holy days
wait to be re-incarnated in our hands.

First, take a look at the eggs, little soldiers
standing to attention in their plastic crate,
white as innocence, waiting for our visions
to happen on their shells. We lift and turn them
in our fingers—elegant, oval—and begin
to pencil in our tracings, like twigs on snow.
The kistkas—the little pens we'll heat over
candle flames—melt black beeswax into

a fluid ink that tentatively follows
the penciled markings—Round One
for our unschooled fingers. "Too bad,
that blot. Try turning it into part of the design."
We learn from it, as from transgression.
Our scrolling continues, unfolds
florid as wrought ironwork, ready
for the first baptism in liquid color.

Say we choose scarlet. The black lines
resist it, but the naked parts turn bright as blood,
inviting further inky intricacies and successive
baths in blue, yellow, green. More tendrils

branch on the ovoid shells. At every stage
the thing looks more confused, chaotic,
incoherent enough to raise anxiety,
an uncertainty about the outcome.

In fact, it looks ugly as death. But wait;
at the end, a slow revelation as we hold our
decorated eggs close to the flames. Rags in hand

we buff the melting wax away, section by section.
Watch now, for the radical surprise
as Sunday's living color replaces the blurred
image, redeems the past.

The promise of Easter comes true.

Collection, Recollection

Can the arrow forget the bow-string
and the bow, their pent-up passion
to let fly, the sudden snap and twang,
the relief of release?

The fledgling, having just
chipped herself free into the nest,
how does she practice
the wide threat of space?

A clear lens, the drop of rain
carries in its orb an image of the sky
from which it fell—a piece of cloud—and
with it a recollection of thunder.

And the predestined satchel
of tomorrow, how can it not be packed
with the finely-orchestrated
chaos of today?

The Golden Carp

All things are parts of a single system called nature;
the individual life is good when it is in harmony with nature.

—Zeno of Citium

The golden carp, over a foot long, glorious,
made more golden by the sun, slides
from under his lily pad towards my shadow,
me standing there by the pond,
watching the water striders, those weightless
navigators of the border between us.

Even under water he must sense
the knife edge between shade and blaze.
His eyes tilt sideways, up, his burnished mouth
lipping, nudging, sampling my air. I am
his fishly dream of the unknown, which he is not
equipped to explore. He is my vision
of existence in an atmosphere thicker than air.

So how? Perhaps that small flip of the tail
is saying, *Hello there!* Can we meet?
Bending, I reach down, finger the surface.
The space between us thins to this sheet
sleek as silk. We share no language but light.

Invasion

Like swoops of dark birds settling, folding huge
wings, anxieties and doubts bend the branches.

Heavy, broody and fidgeting, they've moved in,
building their awkward nests like clots in the trees,

black twigs jutting. Worse than clouds that will pass,
they screen the sky, the stars, any heavenly body.

A clatter rises, intensifies, dense as rifle fire in a war zone,
clogging the air with stabbing, sooty accusations

and arguments that sound irrefutable. It's evident
the intruders plan to take over, reproducing their own

dark-feathered kind, ravenous and predatory,
with orange claws, curved beaks and sheenless wings.

They've driven out the nesting doves, colonizing
all the trees. The whole forest could be next.

I try a clap, and a loud shout, to dislodge them.
Either they can't hear it or they take it for applause.

Their harsh voices promote anarchy, disruption.
They join the local militia. To clear the air, to see

the sun again, I cry for an invasion of
a different kind from beyond *far*, deeper than *in*.

Credo

I believe in Free Enterprise, Pride of Place,
Fiscal Responsibility, The Middle Ages,
Seasonal Allergies, Queen Anne's Lace,
Undying Love, The Communion of Saints,
The Golden Ratio, Due Process, Outer Space,
The Diet of Wurms, The Bay of Fundy,
The Four Seasons, The Commonplace,
The Freedom of the Press, The Milky Way,
The Golden Years, The Human Race,
Pinot Grigio, The Bermuda Triangle,
The Statue of Liberty, Prevenient Grace.

The Possibilities of Clay

for Scott Dillman, on his way to Haiti

There's this bearded man I met
who loves clay. There must be

something of Adam in him, he is
that red, that ready. Between

his firm, clay-colored palms
he rolls glistening balls of the stuff,

each its own small, malleable planet.
Just before firing he thrusts

a wire through each bead—north
to south poles. Kiln-hardened,

they'll each be ready to offer themselves
for decoration—brilliant pigments

in bold and quirky designs
according to the artist's

God-fired imagination. Glazed,
strung on strings, they will become

jewels hurled into the world to show
that humble earth can turn beautiful,

can have worth, can even bring in cash
for those with little else to sell.

To Be a Bird

*"... The birds, taking flight, lift themselves
up to heaven, and instead of hands, spread out
the cross of their wings ..."*–TERTULLIAN

I always wanted to worship
like some high bird, to fly free in prayer
without touching earth, without
the tug of gravity. But my breath
towards heaven is too often
a dry leaf in the wind
that wakes and settles again
as if the emptiness of air
cannot welcome a substance
worth more than a wish.

So, earthbound, I content myself
attending to sky patterns—eagles.
swifts, swallows, even brash
gulls lifting, swooping.
And praise begins to enter me
as I learn to thank God for this
sweet slope, this unkempt green
mountain grass on which I lie,
making a cross with my arms outspread
like a message to heaven.

Architectures

Scaling the Rocks

Yesterday we drove the grandkids to
the Larrabee rocks to breathe the lovely rotting smell
of ocean at low tide. In the crevices that the tide
had left high but not quite dry, pebble jewels
gleamed like amber and silver through lenses of sun
on seawater. Small crabs the color of gravel
scuttled sideways though kelp. Barnacles
clustered like drab dried flowers
along the sandstone shelves on which
our young ones scrambled without fear.

Seven and five—the ages of exploration.
The cries of gulls and children glanced
in our ears like flecks of light. Puget Sound's
purple islands wrap the horizon like scarves knitted
with sequins. Afternoon sun carved
its honeycomb shadows in the sandstone lace,
witness to weather's centuries.

I am not digital, but imprinted by senses
no camera can catch, though my son's Nikon
does its best: Christa and I hunted sea glass
on the pebbled shore, small waves whispered
at its dark, damped edges, far out.

As the sun sank the children tired. We knew that
soon enough the relentless tide would rise
and free the weed and drown the shore
and climb the rocks that always lift
their stony faces to the darkening west.

Three Dimensions

*"... radiance and shadow as far
as the eye can see."*—EAMON GRENNAN

1

The seething sea has rolled
this jagged shard of shale
into a pure ellipse.
Gale has set the gem
high on the brow of the shore,
in a nation of slate-colored
ovals shining
under a skin of rain.

2

When she touches down,
light and poised as a heron,
the dancer leaves a shimmer
in the altitude blurred with
her fresh absence.
Without the impediment
of gravity the dancer
cannot dance.

3

The ragged wounds are still
blotted with dark blood.
Midnight at noon.
The agony, un-forgotten,
carrying its costly dimension
into the flare of paradise—
Christ's indelible shadow
embedded in his glory.

Cave Art

A bulk of beasts, equine, bovine,
inhuman—heads thrust, nostrils flared,
threatening but caught and held
and helpless. Panther, elk, bison,
beings like and unlike ourselves.
And mothers of perpetuity buried,
waiting for our discovery, the
squat females with monstrous breasts
and thighs, wombs of possibility.

When this is all you know
you're drawn to draw it, trapping it
on the darkened walls, cutting
into a rock face, fusing the colors of earth—
ochre, ash, hematite—with stains
of juices—leaves and berries—
to display your fears and visions on
the curving stone.

And with them, something of yourself
that says, I was here. Look—the outlined shape
of my hand! This is what I knew
of beauty and of terror, this
hints at all the other things I could not see
and have to guess at in this darkness.

Unseen

Air is the main thing. The selvage
of landscape and the glistens of water
are merely the floor, or some kind of hem,
an edge of what we can't see.
Now and then clouds form a roof,
a soft ceiling. A cap for the gap.

Open space may rant and rave
invisibly. We feel it, so we are obliged
to name it. Wind.

Why equate visibility
with value? (You, solid in your
purple velvet jacket and heels
may attract attention.
But where would you be
without breath?)

So self-effacing, air, except
in dialog with the visible,
a sigh among leaves,
a moan at the window,
a draft under the door,
a cough in the face.

A suspension of our
disbelief.

Ec-stasis

The music, Gustav Holst's "The Planets,"
is described by the announcer as
moving, touching, powerful. As if,
even as we listen, we'll get shoved
around, displaced, our senses
turning us to another orientation.

So, maybe this is what is meant for us—
to be ready to be unsteady, unhinged,
beside ourselves, constrained by magic
to know the world new, to be
transposed, dislodged, ready for
realignment, reintegration.

Bring whatever it takes—for sight,
for hearing, touch, taste, sense
of smell, spirited imagination, any of
the ways we're engineered
for transformation.

The Moon in Advent

Midnight.
The brilliant disc of a full moon
dodges the sharp edge
of a shifting cloud, stoops,
slides a finger through
the glass skylight,
hard as ice, silted with frost.

Reaches into my room.

No feathers. No sudden fright.
I am not Mary, but this
is a visitation.

In the bedroom, under
the sheet, I lie printed with
the fresh promise of light.

Singing About God in Church

"Unresting, unhasting, and silent as light . . ."

Our attention snags on the words
"silent as light," Does that mean
we take him for granted, the way we barely
notice the morning as it comes up
every day without a sound?

The lake
echoes back silent, its skin
so hushed a mirror for woods and lucid sky
the beauty doubles.

Then in December the sun shrinks away,
filtered through clouds so that
heaven seems drained of life.
And then, maybe, light streaks at us
in a bolt, astonishing us, joining the dark
of heaven with the tree split down its heart,
and the silence of God is broken
in the shock of heaven roaring.

What the Morning Says to Her

Doctor's office. She sits beside me, the sun
from the windows warm on our shoulders,
both of us wait to be called from what is known,
without irony, as the waiting room.

I glance sideways. A wisp of woman,
clearly a lot older than me (and I'm
pretty old) with sparse, nothing-colored
hair, skin drawn tight over cheekbones,

mouth gathered to a thin purse, eyes sparks
of improbable blue. Unexpectedly the purse opens
in a burst of gratitude: "Beautiful sun!
Such a *beautiful* day! It makes me so *happy!*"

She folds me into her smile, enveloping me with
her gift of hilarity. At last my name is called;
I smile back and leave her to her delight,
certain that even should a cloud conceal

the object of her contentment, she'll know that
somewhere it shines up there still. That
no shadow, not even nightfall, can extinguish
the magnificence that inhabits her being.

What to Do with Bits of String

We are expert at extraction, making
something out of something else;
a cat's cradle for the kids. A rag rug.
A torn loaf for turkey stuffing, or Eucharist.
We take traces of a fractured dream
and fashion a plot for a new novel.
Old tires make for resilient highways.
My friend rips out worn sweaters
for new scarves. Women in Africa
roll old magazine pages into beads,
varnishing them for sale in other worlds,
jewels from junk. I rescue river stones
and beach shells for ornaments
along my window sill. They cost nothing.

Try it yourself. See what lovely new thing
God can make from what is common
and discarded. Including your own life.
Call it recycling. Call it renewal
and you're getting at the heart of it.

Soft Rock

You need only to live near mountains
to feel the age in your bones. Take
the sandstone cliffs along our Northwest shore:
looking across pebbled beaches glinting
with sea glass, their faces staring down the ocean,
never as pacific as it sounds. These bluffs
have offered themselves without rest to
the winds, the waters—rising, falling fifteen feet—
the extraordinary tides, rips that tear
water from water, that scour the shores.

On this windless day, I feel joined to
the low shelf on which I sit. Warm
from noon sun, it's pitted into stone lace
by particles whirled by wind for a million years
in the rocks' shallow wounds. Any small grit
will do it, grinding at the stone face, digging deeper,
carving empty eye sockets.

Lines of barnacles like white dried flowers
grow at the waterline, footnotes
to weather's virtuosity.

No one is watching.
Surreptitiously I lean left, touch,
test with my tongue the etched boulder
by my elbow, and taste the sharp salt of storms.
In that brief kiss I think I even sample
the ochre-gray tint of sands that once
laid down their duned lives
to become these rocks of ages.

Trend

October. Five p.m. An autumn-colored sky
the color of my friend Mary's
hair. Like the just-turning-to-flame

leaves on the vine maple
we planted only last year.
A gift surprising as

a birthday cake, even though that's
pretty predictable. The mangoes
in the wooden bowl on the table

match the brilliant color splash
of the bird's head
at the porch feeder.

Even the bright mesh of
the ratty pot-scrubber in my hand
is glory leaking through.

Destination

A visitor from outer space,
this trifling alien flames from
the back hall's dark floor tile
as if this were its target
from the beginning.

Damaged from entry,
a crumpled tissue of flicker,
it has never landed in this spot
before—this lozenge of light.

I trace the trajectory back
and back through slats,
window glass, a screen,
out beyond atmosphere to find
its source. Everything
has a source.

Carved by shadows,
complications of alder leaves,
hills, mist, cloud, light years.

And now, here, this
trifling signal—the sun's emissary
with its slow wink.

Lakeway Drive

Frost has chewed
the blacktop all winter.
Pitted with wear, old tar is peeling
from last year's patched cracks.

Driving to town
I learn to avoid pot-holes the size
of buckets and shallow graves, wondering
if our Whatcom County Budget
allows for extensive repairs. Pray
they don't just bandage it again.

Soon enough I myself will degrade
into a dirt road unless
mending happens, unless
some re-construction machine
lumbers up to work on me.

Now and then
I tear the dressings
off my own wounds
to see how the scars are doing.

It makes me think,
maybe, if a new surface is laid,
glistening and striped,
I should think of getting
a fresh tattoo.

What I Needed to Do

I made for grief a leaden bowl
      and drank it, every drop.
And though I thought I'd downed it all
      the hurting didn't stop.

I made of hope a golden sieve
      to drain my world of pain.
Though I was sure I'd bled it dry
      the void filled up again.

I made of words a silver fork
      and stabbed love in the heart,
and when I found the sweetness gone
      I chewed it into art.

Verb

A poem dredges for meanings
from the mud at the bottom of a
tidal mind.

A word—an eyelash, a nipple, a toenail,
an earlobe—a scrap attached to
something larger.

Letters strung together
turn strong enough to kick open a door or
nudge it closed with one finger.

It takes only a coin or a thumbnail to block
the sun. A fly on the glass. A tree twig.
The slat of a window blind.

In the shadow cave, the sudden
spark of a single candle
heightens the mystery.

How well the world could work without me.
What reason is there for any of us to be
thrust into being by a word?

Under Cover

We see God in the shape
he shows us. For some, fire.
For others, holy smoke, oil,
running river, sheep's crook,
muscular right arm that holds
against the dark, the dread.

It is the oddity of poets
to not see the world straight on
but at some slant, under the skin,
behind the scrim—a scurry
of leaves, clouds. God
speaks his presence in
the wind, in frost.

I sensed him even in the ink
warming inside my pen before
these words arrived.

States of Being

Isn't stability greatly
      over-rated?
Why would I ever want to sit
      still and smug as a rock,
      confident, because of my great
      weight, that I will not
      be moved?
Better to be soft as water,
      easily troubled, with
      at least three modes
      of being, able to shape-
      shift, to mirror, to cleanse,
      to drift downstream,
To roar when I encounter
      the rock.

Singularities

For every memory lost
there will be one
that will not let go.

Like a phone ringing,
you can't
not answer it.

*

To write a poem is
to fling a stone,
not sure where
it will land.

The best ones come
when the poet
is taken
by surprise, when

that random pebble
of an image
discovers
its true home.

*

Brief, like breath
on a mirror,
the variable
ghosts on the bay,
dip and lift.

Sailing, to find the breeze,
you steer towards
the far, dark cat's paw

not sure if
it will still be there
when you are.

Compline at the Cathedral

St. Mark's Cathedral, Seattle

Late evening, and the students stroll in,
silent, gangly, some barefoot as Moses at
the burning bush. But in this dim,
deep space the only fire is a candle burning,
and a cross, lit dimly. The young
spread their blankets in the aisles
and around the altar and lie on their backs,
listening up, seeming to be at home
with holiness. I see hands raised for praise,
but some seem simply to doze,
a flock at rest in their pasture.

Oh, to be young again, in cut-offs and cargoes,
looking not at each other but to the unseen
through a canopy of chanted, translucent sound.
At this evening's completion I pray that they
will carry this benediction with them
into Seattle's dark, unquiet streets.

Spire

Sunday. My car aims for church
up rain-wet Holly Street. Against the sky
the steeple carves its point, a sailor's beacon
for navigating Bellingham Bay.
The steeple shape brings to mind the word
spire. Thinking of its source my questions
rise (a root that must have split
and multiplied, as language does,
to cense and drift apart like smoke).

From *spire* I first suppose some kind
of breath that spirals up like
the grey ghost that lifts from
a snuffed wick. I know of *suspiration*,
a kind of skyward exhalation, a poignant
sigh—sometimes a prayer sharp enough
to rattle heaven, a spiky wire
to jiggle in the lock and open
paradise's gates.

Later, from the OED, I read of *spiration*,
the Spirit's own creative breath,
and later, down the page, surprising,
a bolt from the blue—*spire*, from *spear*,
a spike, a stalk, a sharply-tapered blade,
a point for penetration.

I will aspire, therefore, to worship God
in spirit, in the Spirit. And that's, I guess,
the point of inspiration.

Dancing in the Cathedral

The bell-ringers rise and
fall with the weight of their bells,
holding on for dear life to the pulls,
the ropes rough in their hands,
the young ones lifted up, up
from the belfry floor like
adolescent angels treading air,
as if so caught up in those
peals of sound—each of them in turn
answering the plea of ponderous metal—
they rise like feathers in a wind.

Consecrated, cassocked, gathered
for this task of intricate rhythm-ing,
they learn to weave their way through
the ring-patterns like pigeons to
the dovecote over the cadences
of distance. Even a mile away we
ourselves sway like bells, snared
by the tolling, its cords of holy dance.

Epiphany

At Jesus' baptism "the heavens were torn open."
—MARK 1 & PSALM 29

We may feel safe in our beds,
but heaven, say the Celts,
is three feet away, just
the other side of recognition.
Like consciousness, it presses
down on us, even during
sleep—a lucent cloud.

Yet after dreams of glory
and thunder, we wake
to the commonplace—rain,
an urgent phone call from
across town, trepidations
and small terrors, hard-edged
bits of equipment,
the mingled smell
of roses and salt hay.

How to be aware
of every dimension!

Closer than breath, watch for
the bevies of angels who dust our lives
with prisms, huge splendors
swarming the gap.

With a fury of feathers,
tear open that near, teeming heaven.
Strip our oaks to writhing,
our cedars to ripping and shattering.
Like the flames of fire, quicken us with

Voice. Articulate unspeakable things
into our sudden hearing. Dazzle
our newly-opened eyes.

Mary Considers Her Situation

What next, she wonders,
with the angel disappearing, and her room
suddenly dark.

The loneliness of her news
possesses her. She ponders
how to tell her mother.

Still, the secret at her heart burns like
a sun rising. How to hold it in—
that which cannot be contained.

She nestles into herself, half-convinced
it was some kind of good dream,
she, its visionary.

But then, part dazzled, part prescient—
she hugs her body, a pod with a seed
that will split her.

Advent III

for Marya Gjorgiev

The third week, and about now
Mary is heavy with God, her first
and the Father's only, with a journey
to plan for, going south. Anxiety
is in the air. It is so dark and cold
and kind Joseph is only a man, not
a midwife. She feels answerable
for the welfare of the heaving life
in her belly. For her, for us,
Advent speaks of adventure.

Let us feel with Mary in her
waiting and knowing. And not
knowing. Today I try to remember
all the world's mothers and every
new child yet to arrive, made
in the same God-likeness. Pray
for more than a cave in the hill town
when their time comes. Though that
will do if there is love enough.

Getting It Right

Jesus might have died
a dozen times before he died.

An incidental death—tetanus
from a nail, a splinter.

A baptismal drowning.
A drink from a tainted well.

Rotten fish.
Desert starvation.

A stoning, a sudden
push over the edge,

or a falling overboard in a storm.
A choking by a demon on the loose,

a bar room brawl
at the local pub.

So when it happened, it seemed
like someone

got it right. Right time,
right reason,

for God to let it
happen.

Iron

Here, take a look at this old nail. Rust
reddens it almost to the glow
into which it was once forged, hammered
over and over, in great heat.

We recognize its shape and use—
icon-ed by the furnace of centuries.
Pointed for piercing, length variable,
jutting arrow-straight, the struck end blunted
to halt the thrust and stumble
into wood hard as an old bone
or yielding as green fir.

I lift it in my hand to look, to test
its metal chill on my skin.
But still, in the mind it bites
through tendoned palm to solid beam
like stabbing a ripe fruit. Like opening
a vein to stain my whole being
with someone else's blood.

Emmaus Road Remembered

My camera's eye waits to secure
whatever comes in view, to catch and hold
small chronicles of glint and shape and shine
and subtle shadings in its blunt black
box. Each of them holds their breath until
a kind of resurrection happens on a screen.
Some esoteric magic translates them into sharp details
to see again, and show to friends.

Trust needs to know that sounds and sights
and words imprinted later, tell the truth.
So what about that couple, part of a holy triad
walking and listening, stopping for evening hunger—
did they get it right when they remembered?
Did they play with the crumbs, wondering?
How cleanly did they gather those husks,
memorials of loaf and life and resurrected bread?
Did they agree? And how perfectly did they later
tell the story for our distant ears?

Secure

"I will hold you in the palm of my hand."

To find shelter,
(the song says)
in the palm
of God, you need
to inhabit
its fissures—
the life and death
lines, the cracked
skin, the calluses
thickened
from long labor
with wood,
the generosity
of healing touch,
the skill for all that
Creation, all those
generous cures,
but deepest,
the open
bloody hole
in which
your wrong
is drowned.

Translation

After resurrection, Jesus acted strange,
materializing through solid wood,
even though he didn't look
that different. The gashes seeped still,
varnishing the tentative hand, the fingers

that needed to know him new.
Let me say how strange I feel,
trusting this to be true—that a body
can be both mortally wounded and
whole enough to dodge decay,

as though, half-emptied already
of corporeality, half-way to heaven,
his hands were still bony enough
to gut a couple of lake fish and grill them,
taking multiplication the next step.

Of course, he was always more
than one thing at once—utterly one and
utterly other, now dissolving into
thin air, now re-assembling anywhere
in some new tongue of flame.